The market at this time is saturated with similarly botched and badly written skits on vintage children's literature. However, Dung Beetle can make the solemn guarantee that this is the most botched and badly written book of any style or era, and we are prepared to back that guarantee with a solid gold promise. If any reader should be disappointed in the scale of their disappointment, Dung Beetle will offer an unlimited quantity of Dung Beetle Vouchers, which are not redeemable in any high street or online stores.

This book belongs to:

NEW WORDS is a new experimental learning scheme exclusive to Dung Beetle Books, where children are given stepping stones to the interior meaning of a surface text. These come in the form of three key words, each of which give a clue to the author's deeply sinister intent. Eventually, your child will learn to confuse insight with paranoia, and so develop a healthy, progressive mind.

Book 1d

THE DUNG BEETLE NEW
WORDS READING SCHEME

We do

Christmas

by
M. ELIA and E. ELIA
with illustrations by
M. ELIA

Printed in Poland by EU compliant elves

First edition, 2018

It is Christmas Eve, and we are going out to buy presents.

"I like those shoes," says Susan.

"You like smoking the crack pipe of consumer capitalism," says Mummy.

"No, I like those shoes," says Susan.

"Are you offended by the Christmas tree?" asks Mummy.

"I am not offended," says the Imam.

"I am offended that you are not offended," says Mummy.

"That's the baby Jesus," says John

"He died so that we could go shopping" says Mummy.

We are home.
Mummy has turned on
the Christmas lights.

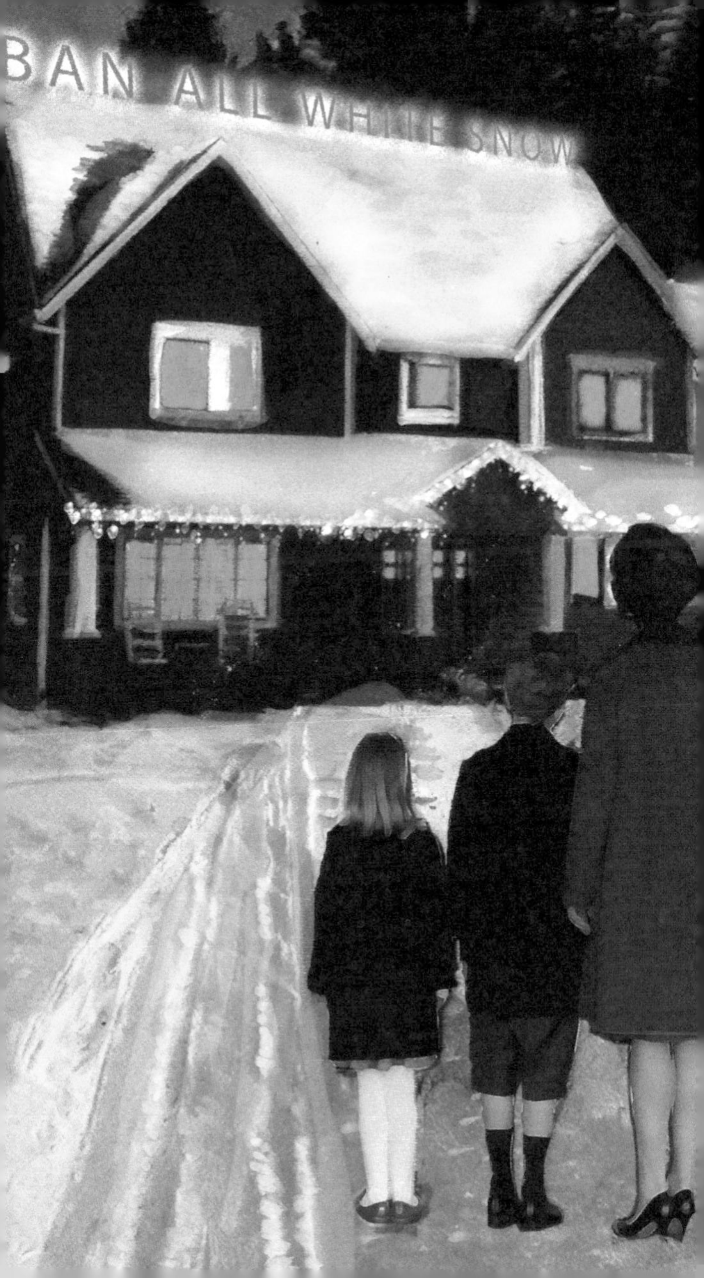
BAN ALL WHITE SNOW

"Is Father Christmas real?" asks John.

"Yes," says Mummy, "he is a real marketing ploy."

"I love marketing ploys," says Susan.

It is 3am.

John and Susan have been woken up.

There are loud voices in the living room.

Mummy is arguing with Santa.

Now we are looking at Santa's list.

There are many names on it.

"Is that my name?" asks Jane.

"No," says Santa, "your name is listed under Children of the Morally Bankrupt."

"Stick your morals," says Mummy.

"Come with me," says Santa, "I will show you the magic of Christmas."

"And I will show you the magic of deconstructivism," says Mummy.

"I will deconstruct your deconstructivism," says Santa.

"Shut up," says Mummy.

new words

clever   clever   Derrida

"Is this Rudolph or Dasher?" asks Susan.
"This is an Uber Reindeer," says Santa.

"I have an app on my Santa-Phone, which sources any freelance reindeer in the vicinity. I think his name is Mahmoud."

.

"How does the sleigh fly?" asks John.

"Mahmood has a massive jet turbine installed in his bum," says Santa.

"Is this your workshop?" asks John.

"Yes," says Santa, "although we have relocated much of our manufacturing base to Bangladesh, because it has fewer elf health and safety laws."

"We are diversifying our brand identity," says Santa, "so that we can appeal to a more sustainable, multi-platform consumer base.'

"What does that mean?" says Susan.

"I don't know," asks Santa

new words   aimless   word   party

"What are the elves doing?" asks Mummy.

"They are writing algorithms which will monitor children's online behaviour," says Santa, "though I cannot tell you why."

We are at the airport.

Mahmoud's bum is broken.

Santa has got us cheap tickets home.

We are home now.

"Why is there nothing inside our presents?" asks John.

"Check your privilege," says Mummy.

"Where is that?" asks John.

new words   gift   of   guilt

Here are Santa's presents.

John has a gun.

Susan has a doll.

Mummy is writing an angry letter to The Guardian.

It is Boxing Day.

Mummy has tied Santa to a chair.

She is forcing him to watch correctional videos.

"Can I go now?" asks Santa

"Once I have dismantled your patriarchal superiority complex" says Mummy.

"OK," says Santa.

new words   soapy   santa   brain

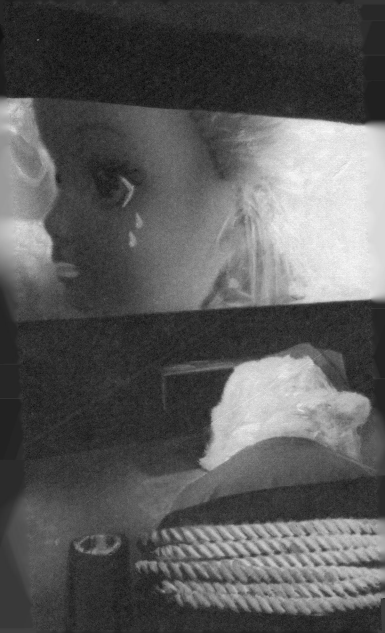

Where is Santa?

"He is in the special learning room,'" says Mummy.

"I don't want to die in there," says Jane.

"You wont, so long as you feel the right things," says Mummy.

We have written our
New Years resolutions.

"I will give up sweets',"
says Peter
"I will study harder,"
says Jane
"I will adopt a refugee,"
says Mummy.
"You said that last year,"
says John.

new words   empty   gesture   dance

New words used in this book

Total number of new words 60

First published 2018 ©

The History of Dung Beetle books

Dung Beetle are an educational publishing house founded in 1936 in Dunging, a small English village renowned for the high quality of its manure. Originally set up by a family of retired Presbyterian manure workers, the founders set out to deliver to children's publishing the same fine standards of workmanship and attention to detail they once did to dung.

Dung Beetle's first success came in 1938 with the publication of *Why We Burn Books,* an early learning guide to fascism, which sold particularly well in Central and Eastern Europe. Later notable publications include *Blitzkrieg for the Under 5s, Let's Learn about Radiation Sickness, There's an Immigrant in My Cafe*, and *Let's Go in the Strange Man's Car.*
Dung Beetle continue to produce high quality books and early learning tools which cover a range of sensitive or difficult topics. Their key goal is simple: to embed core literacy and numeracy skills into children's first knowledge of evil and death.

Est doctrina de stercore*

*From shit comes learning

For just as the humble Dung Beetle gathers faeces from the forest floor in which to lay its eggs, the child lays 'eggs of knowledge' in the turd of its own mind.